HAL•LEONARD®
HARMONICA PLAY-ALONG

POP CLASSICS

AUDIO
ACCESS
INCLUDED

PLAYBACK+
Speed • Pitch • Balance • Loop

T0081522

To access audio visit:
www.halleonard.com/mylibrary

Enter Code
4025-7963-7234-8186

Chromatic Harp by Will Galison
Chord and Bass Harps by George Miklas

ISBN 978-1-4234-2610-3

HAL•LEONARD®
7777 W. BLUEMOUND RD. P.O. BOX 13819 MILWAUKEE, WI 53213

Dear fellow harmonica players,

Playing jazz on the chromatic harmonica is one of the great pleasures of my life, and with this volume, I hope I can help you develop your skills and your enjoyment of this endlessly engaging pursuit.

In this volume you will find two versions of each song. The first is of me playing along with the rhythm section tracks; the second is just the rhythm tracks without me, for you to play over.

In my performances, I have attempted to demonstrate some of the principles of jazz interpretation and improvisation that are important to me. Some of these are:

Tone

Because playing jazz on the harmonica is such a challenge in itself, some players overlook the importance of the overall tone they produce. Good harmonica tone is produced by proper embouchure (mouth position) and breathing technique. Using an appropriate microphone—with EQ and effect for amplifying and/or recording—is important, but it will not make up for weak acoustic tone.

Interpretation of Melody

One good way for beginners to approach improvisation is simply to interpret the melody in a personal way. The melodies on these recordings are all played with my personal interpretation, but I encourage you to play the melodies as you feel them. While it's important to play the correct notes of the original melody, your phrasing and ornamentation of those notes is largely what defines your unique style as a jazz musician.

For beginning improvisers, embellishment of the melody can be a first step, which does not require a deep knowledge of jazz harmony. Just follow your ear, and your emotions.

Playing Technique and Phrasing

While teaching harmonica technique is outside the scope of the book, the harmonica tablature can give a good idea of how I executed the more challenging passages in my improvisations. Because there are alternate ways of playing Fs and Cs on the chromatic, many phrases can be played in several different ways. I took care to play my improvisations in the most efficient and musical way I could, and these choices are reflected in the tablature. If a phrase seems very difficult to play, try following the tablature; it may become easier.

Learning which F and which C to play in a particular passage is an important part of harmonica technique. The "blow and draw" action of the harmonica makes playing smooth legato lines a real challenge. Finding the most efficient way to play the alternate Fs and Cs can help avoid a "choppy" phrasing.

Finally, while you are very welcome to learn and perform my entire solos if they appeal to you, the real point of this book/audio package is to help you evolve your own "voice" on the instrument. I hope that my solos will show you some ideas that I came up with, and inspire you to discover your own. Although it may seem constrained by its unusual design and playing technique, the harmonica is capable of far more musical nuance and virtuosity than we can imagine.

—Will Galison

POP CLASSICS

CONTENTS

Page	Title
4	Bluesette TOOTS THIELEMANS
12	Cherry Pink and Apple Blossom White JERRY MURAD'S HARMONICATS
30	From Me to You THE BEATLES
16	Love Me Do THE BEATLES
20	Midnight Cowboy from MIDNIGHT COWBOY
24	Moon River from BREAKFAST AT TIFFANY'S
28	Peg o' My Heart JERRY MURAD'S HARMONICATS
33	A Rainy Night in Georgia BROOK BENTON
38	CHROMATIC HARMONICA NOTATION LEGEND

Bluesette

Words by Norman Gimbel
Music by Jean Thielemans

5

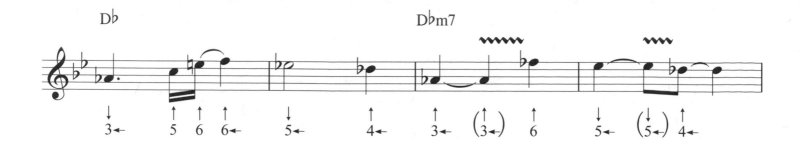

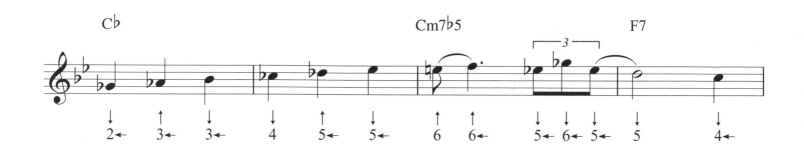

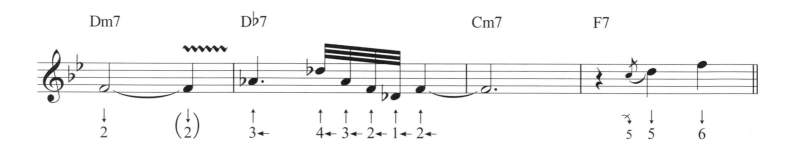

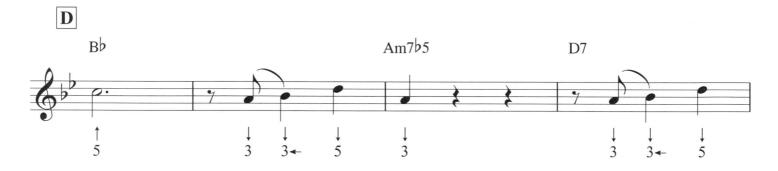

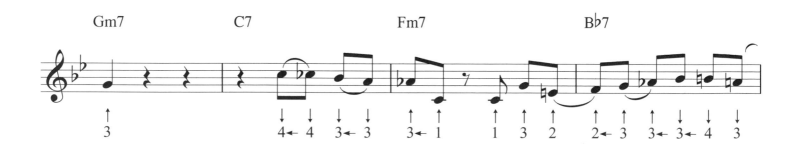

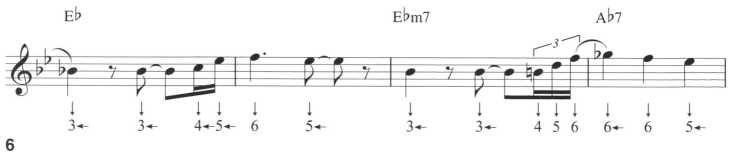

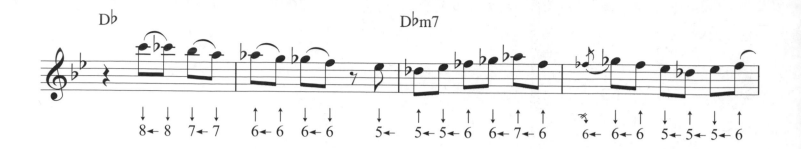

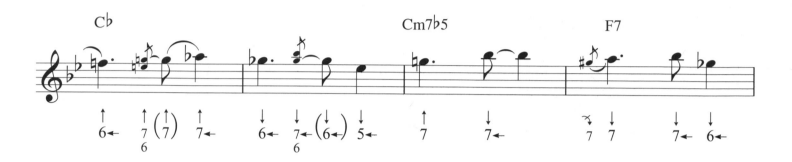

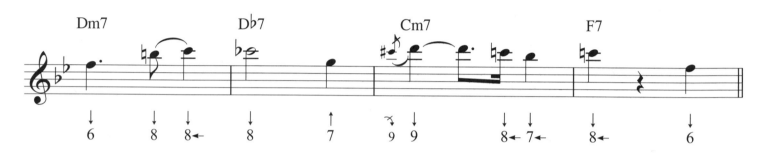

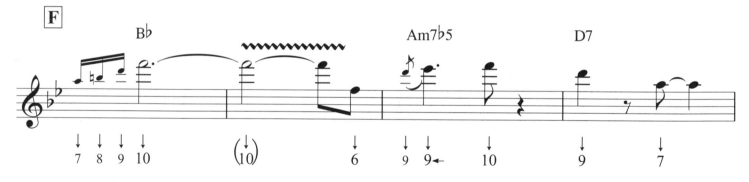

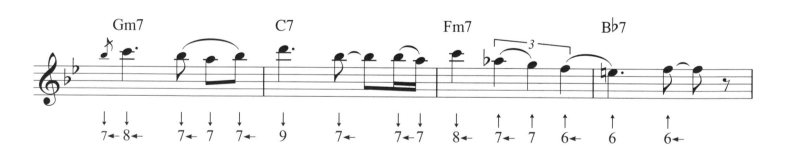

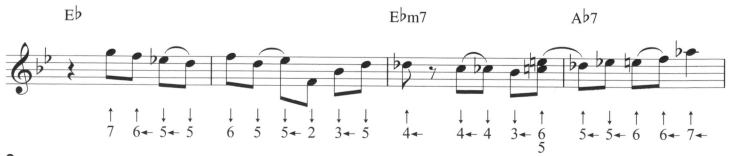

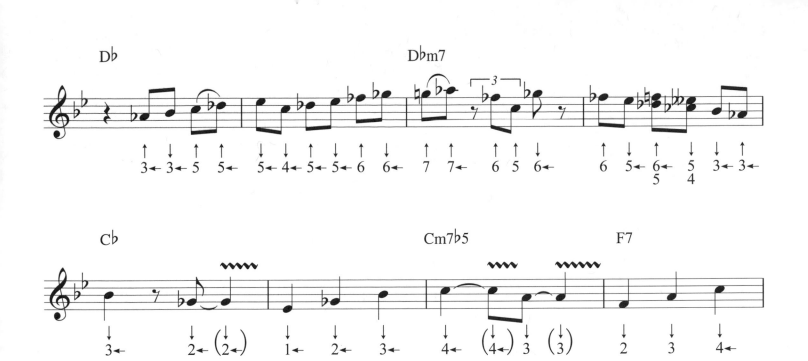

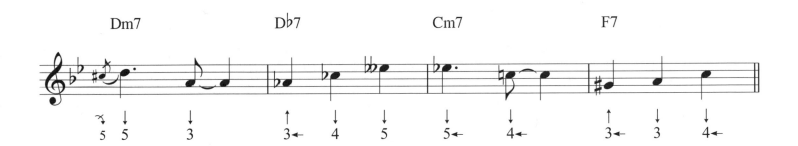

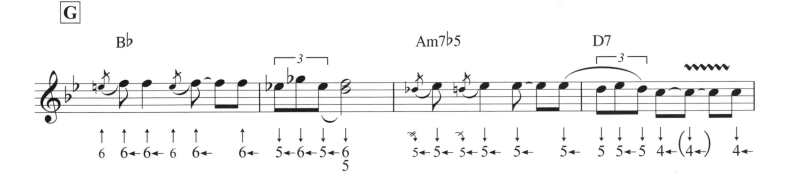

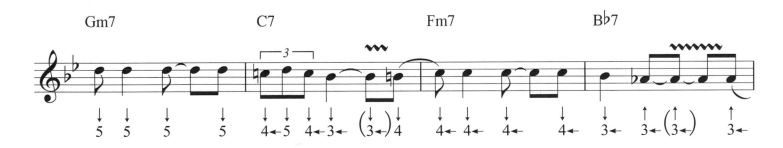

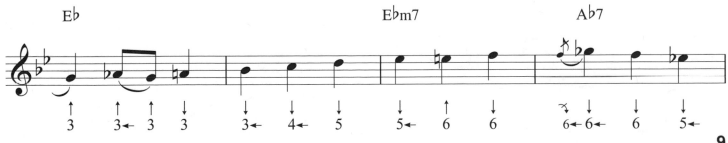

11

Cherry Pink and Apple Blossom White

from UNDERWATER
French Words by Jacques Larue
English Words by Mack David
Music by Marcel Louiguy

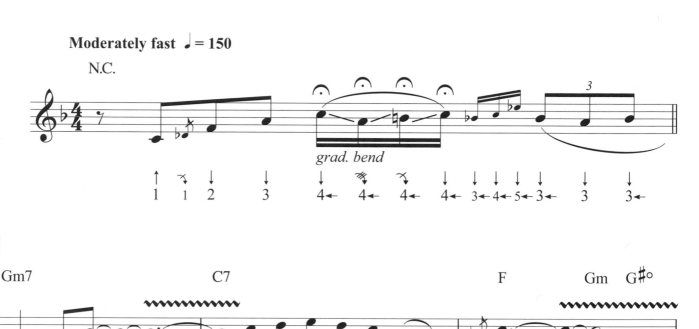

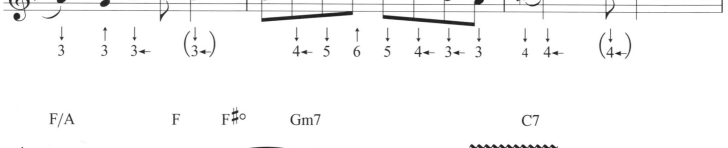

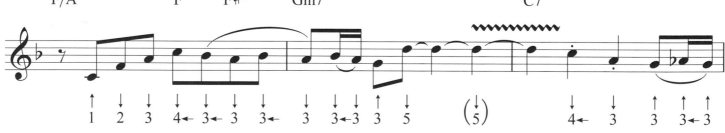

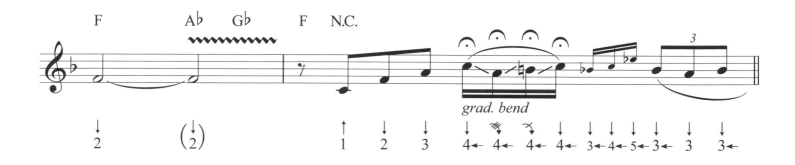

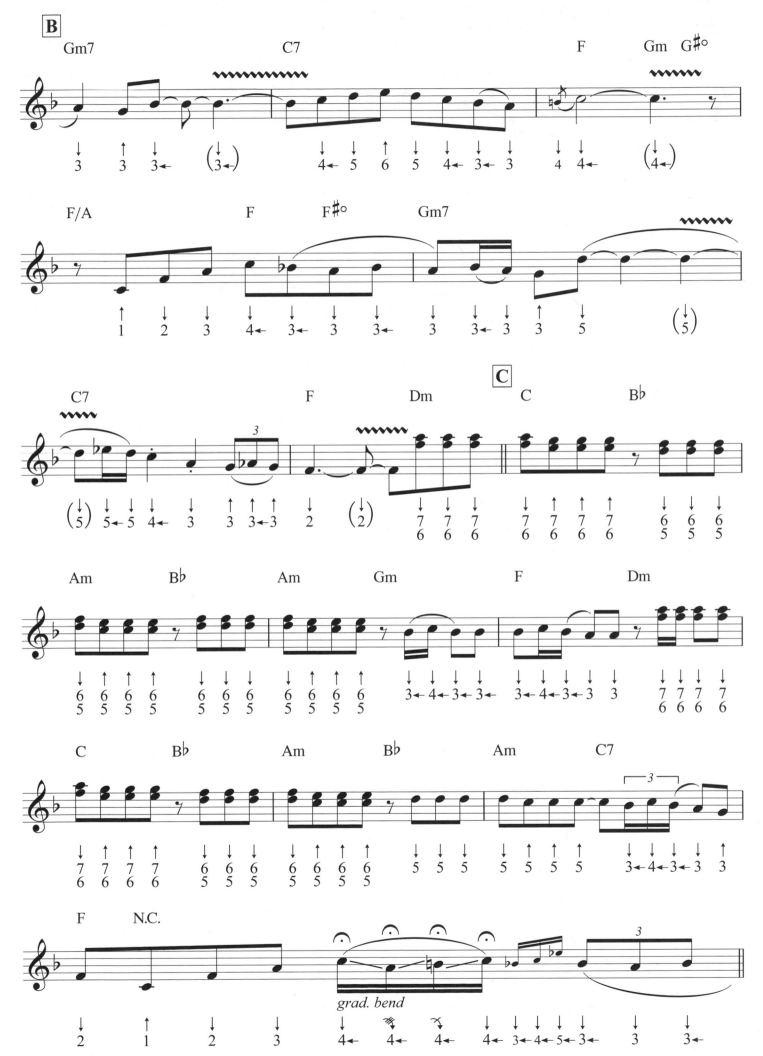

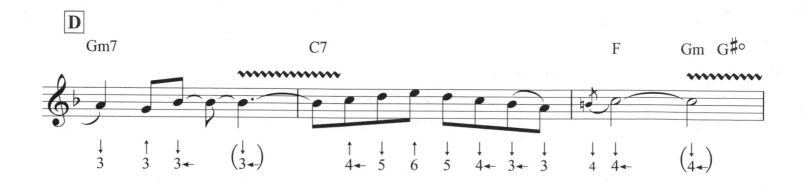

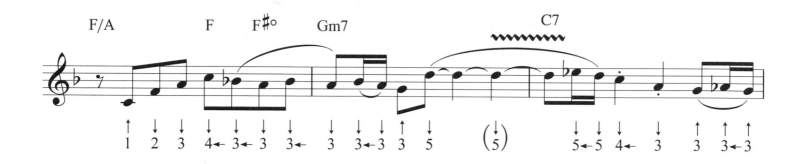

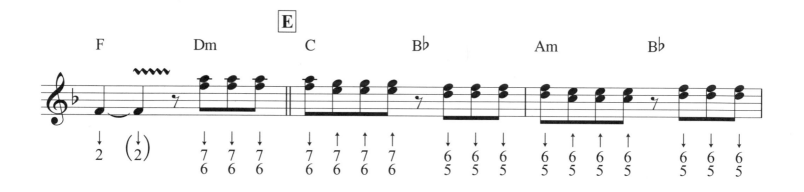

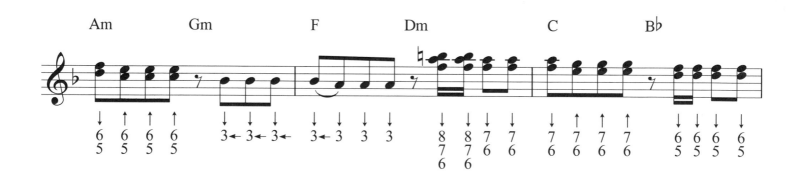

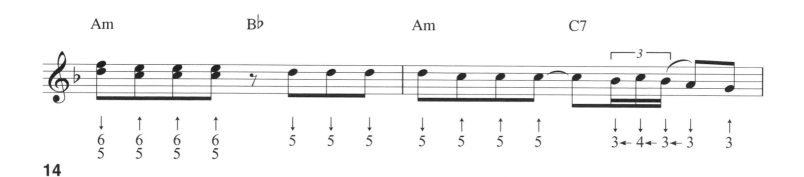

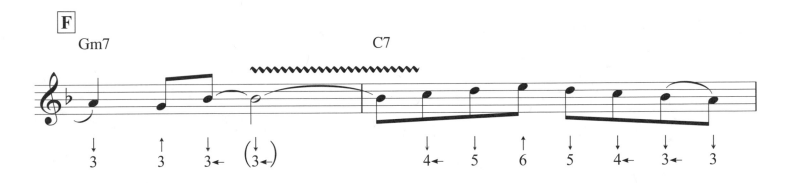

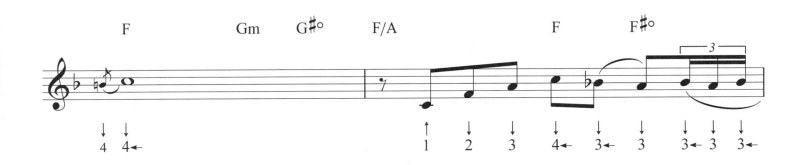

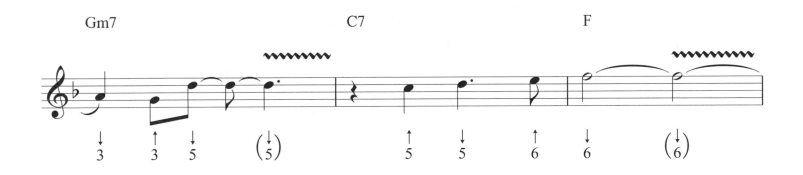

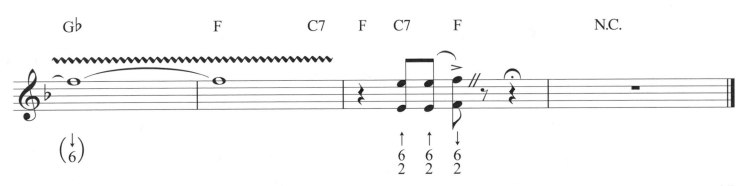

Love Me Do

Words and Music by John Lennon and Paul McCartney

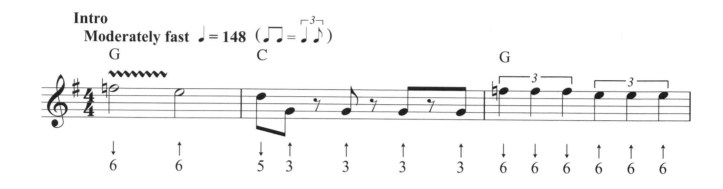

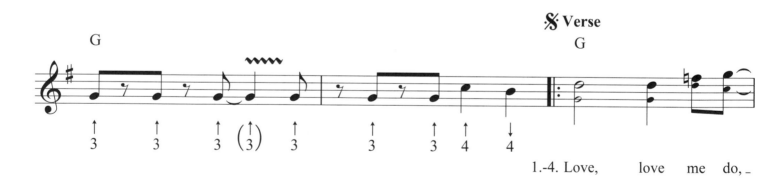

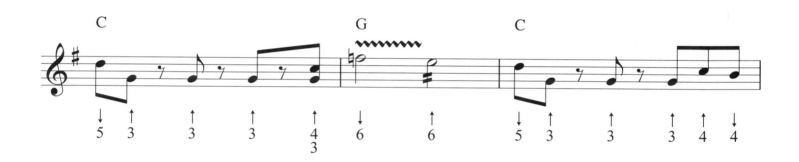

1.-4. Love,   love   me   do, ___

___   you   know   I   love   you. ___   I'll   al - ways   be   true, ___

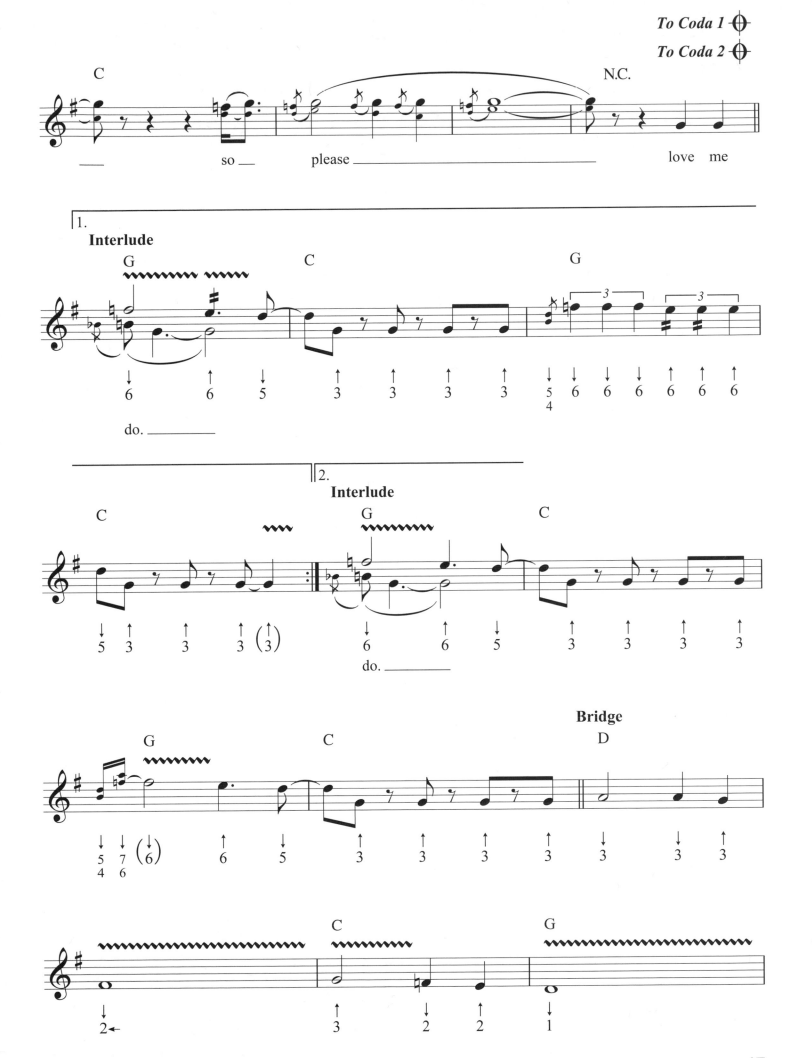

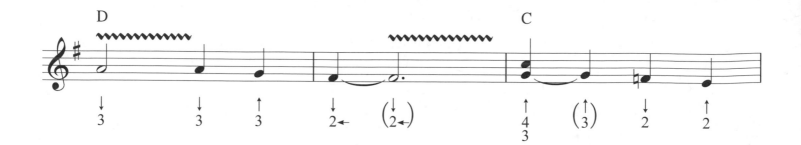

D.S. al Coda 1   ⊕ **Coda 1**

Interlude

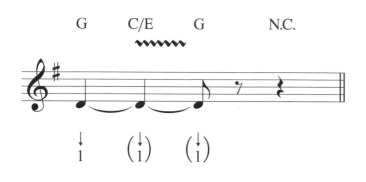

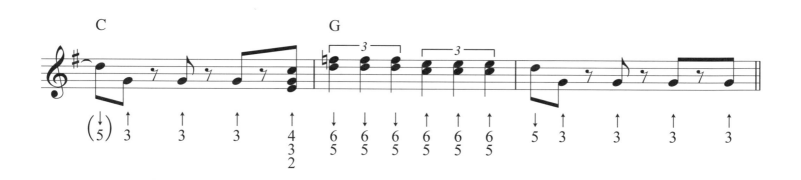

Harmonica Solo

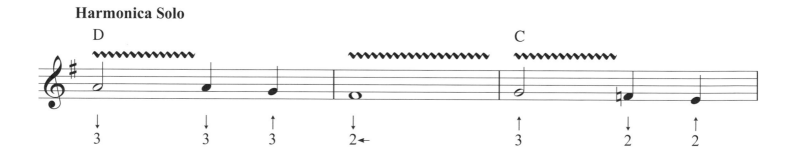

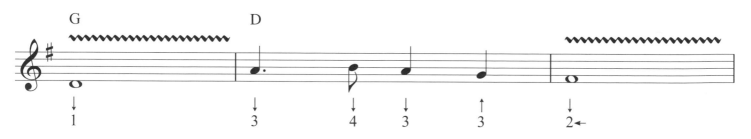

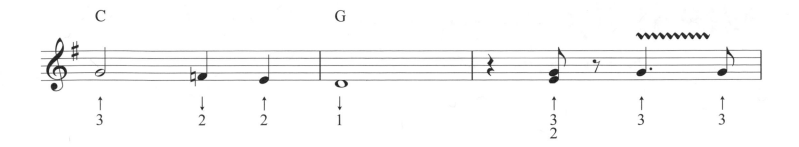

D.S. al Coda 2

 Coda 2

Outro

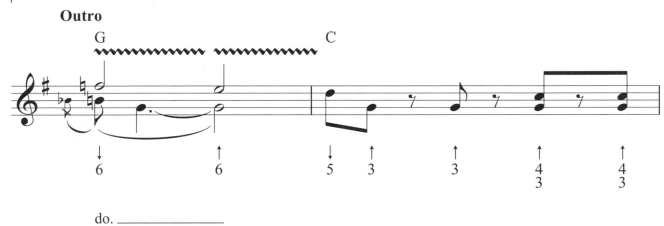

do. _____

Begin fade

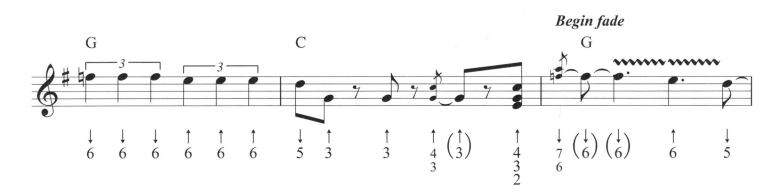

Fade out

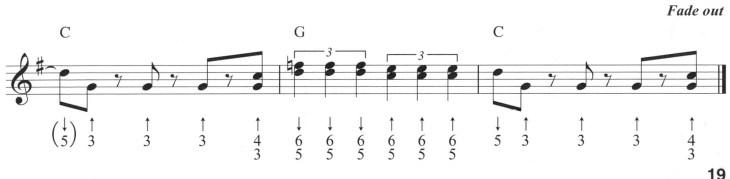

Midnight Cowboy

from the Motion Picture MIDNIGHT COWBOY
Music by John Barry
Lyric by Jack Gold

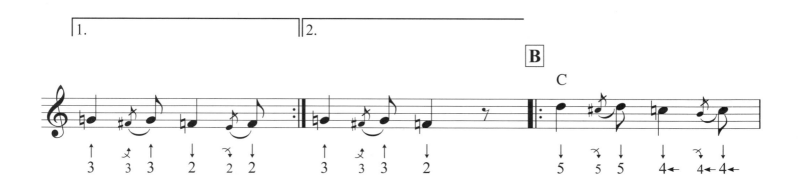

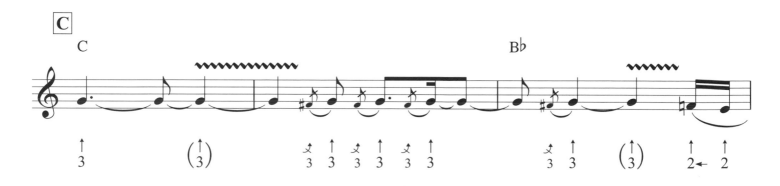

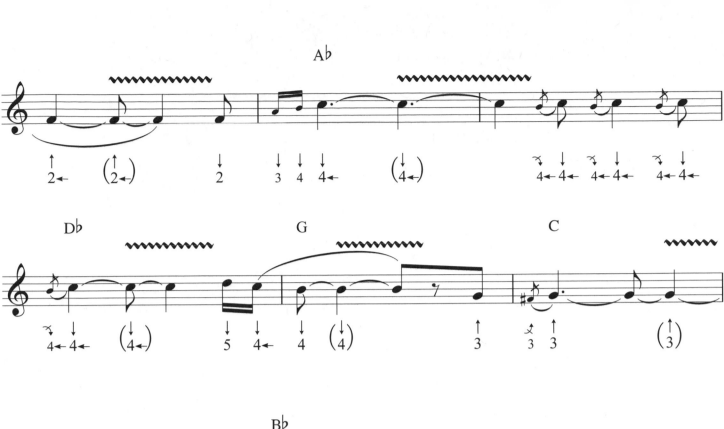

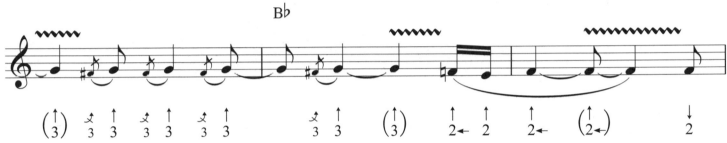

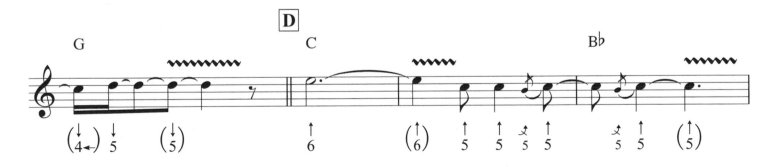

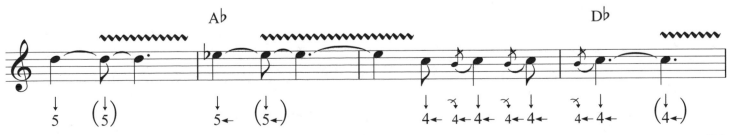

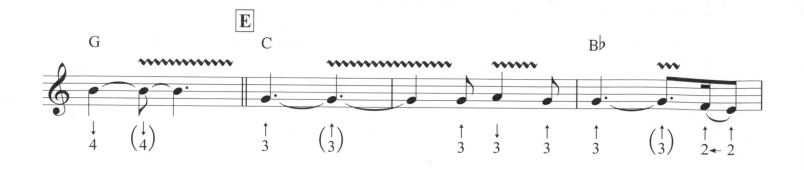

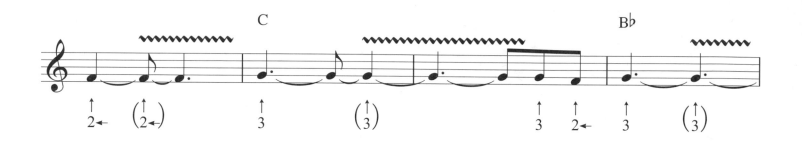

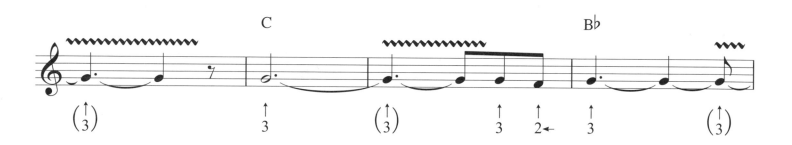

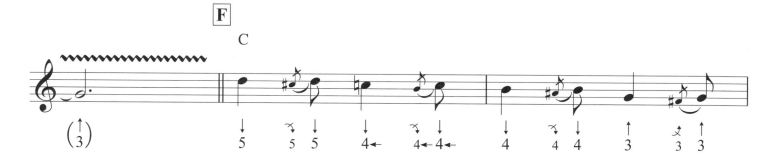

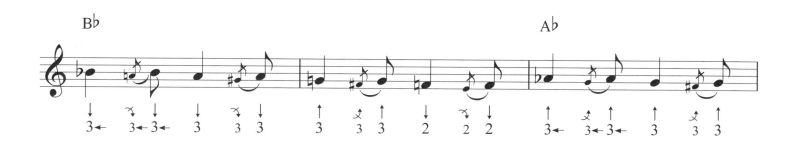

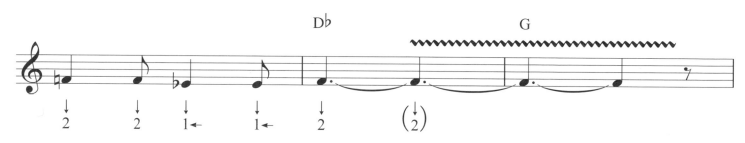

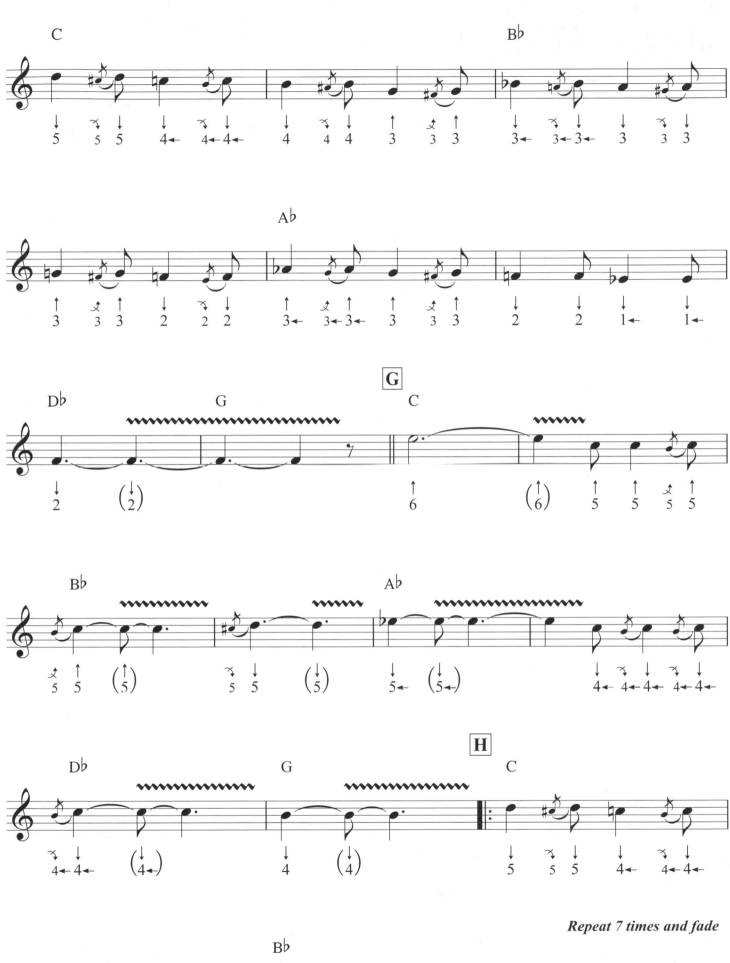

Repeat 7 times and fade

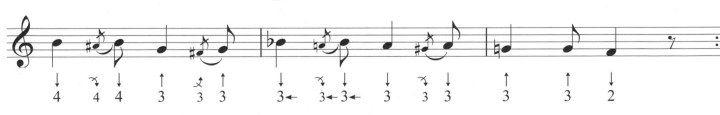

Moon River

from the Paramount Picture BREAKFAST AT TIFFANY'S
Words by Johnny Mercer
Music by Henry Mancini

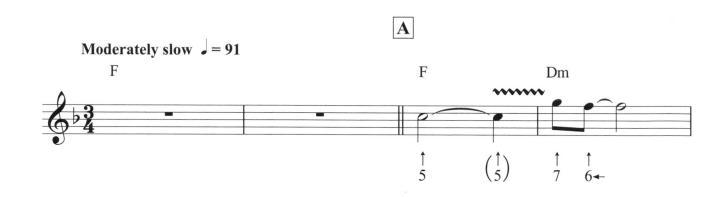

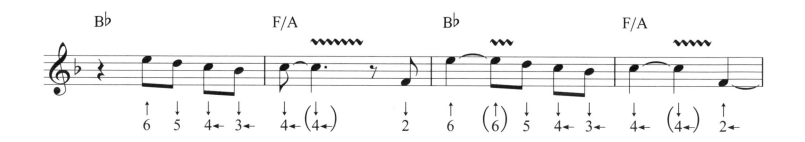

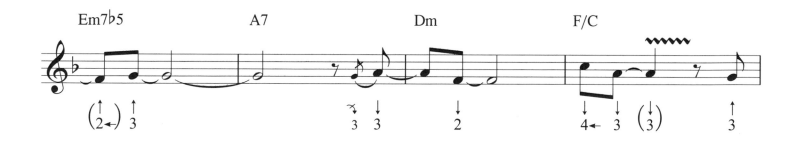

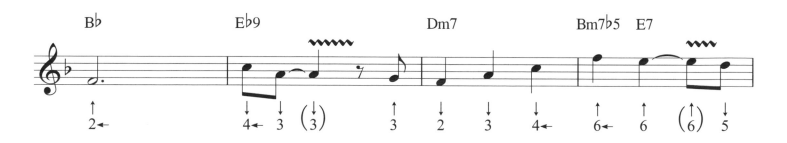

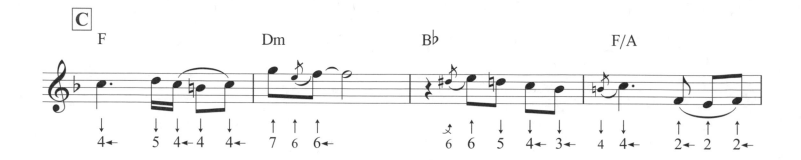

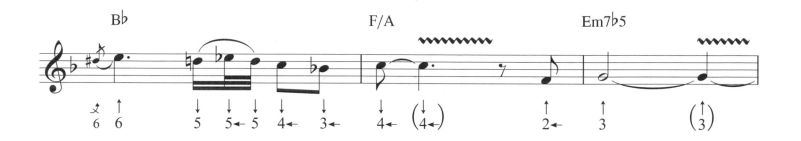

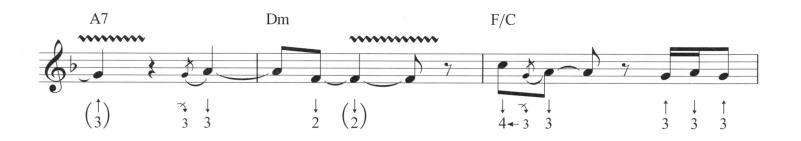

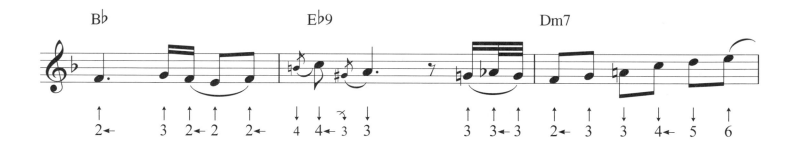

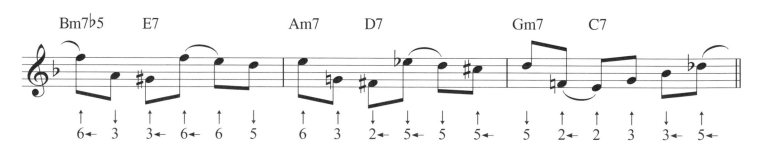

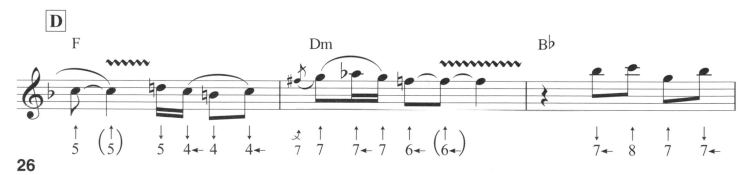

26

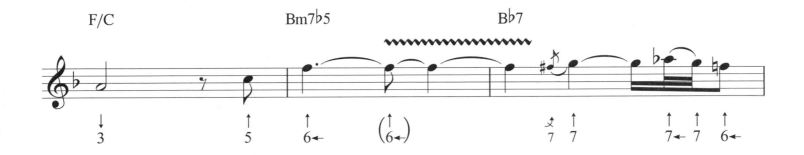

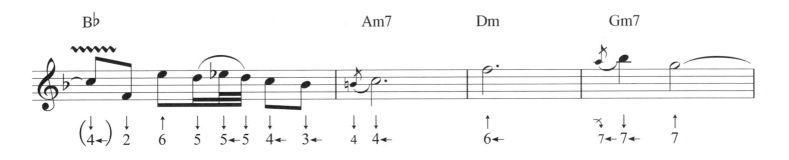

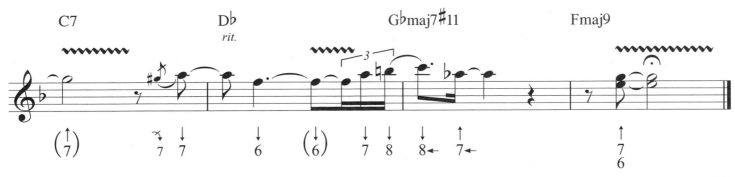

Peg o' My Heart

Words by Alfred Bryan
Music by Fred Fisher

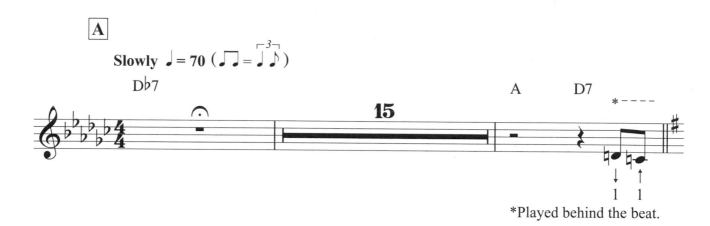

*Played behind the beat.

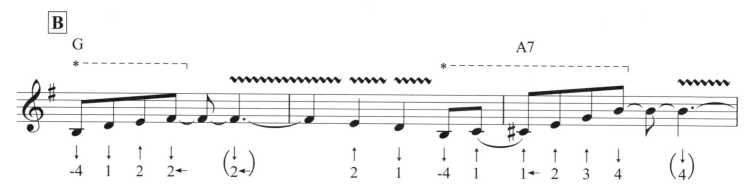

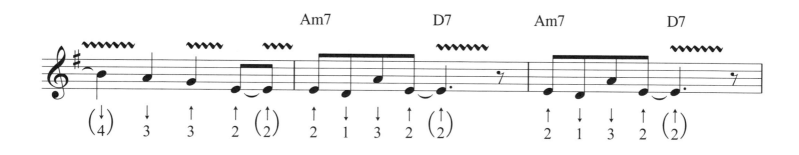

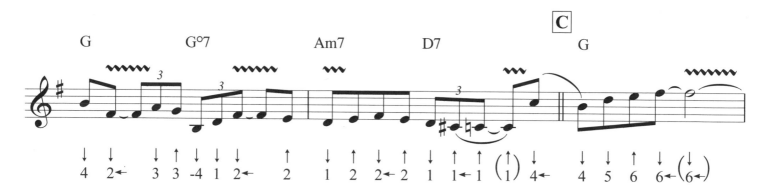

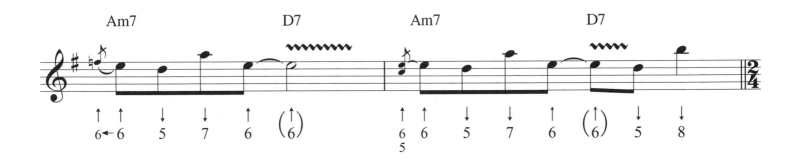

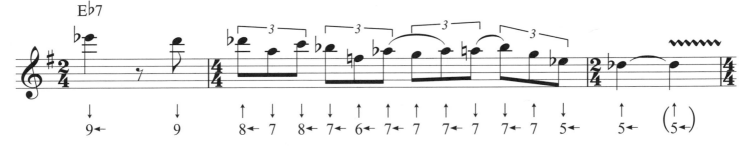

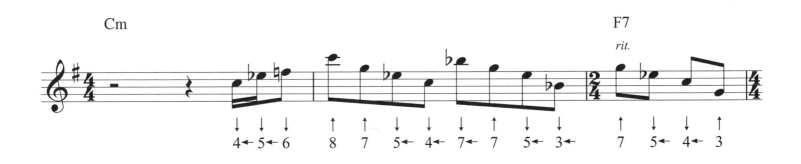

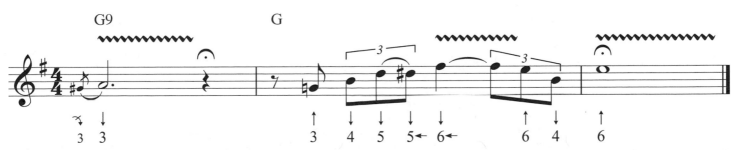

From Me to You

Words and Music by John Lennon and Paul McCartney

31

Just call on me ___ and I'll send it a - long ___ with love, ___

Bridge

___ from me ___ to you. ___ I got arms that long to

hold ___ you and keep you by my ___ side. I got

lips that long to kiss ___ you and keep you sat - is -

D.S. al Coda   ⊕ **Coda**

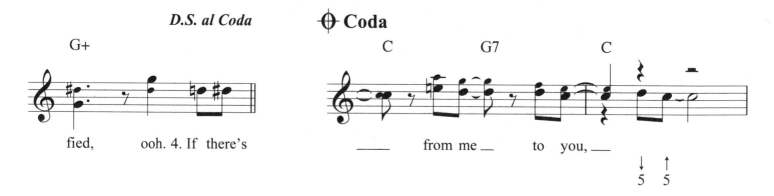

fied, ooh. 4. If there's ___ from me ___ to you, ___

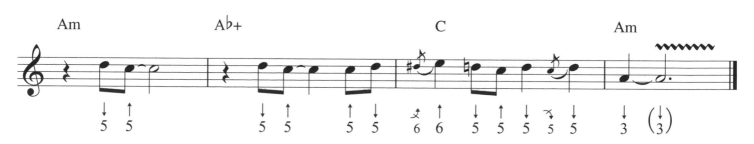

A Rainy Night in Georgia

Words and Music by Tony Joe White

Em   G   Dmaj7

like it's rain - in' all o - ver the world. ___   I feel ___

Cmaj7   Dmaj7

___ like it's ___ rain - in' all _____ o - ver the world. ___

Verse

Dmaj7   G

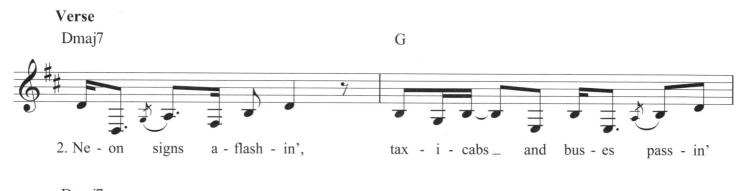

2. Ne - on signs a - flash - in', tax - i - cabs ___ and bus - es pass - in'

Dmaj7

    3   2   2   2←   3   4   5   6←   6← 6← 6← 6← (6←) 6   5   6   3

through the night. ___   A

                             G

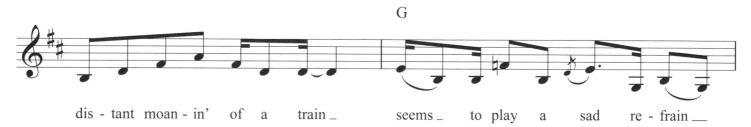

dis - tant moan - in' of a train ___ seems ___ to play a sad re - frain ___

Dmaj7

     5   6← 6← 7   8   7   7   8   7   6←

to the night.

35

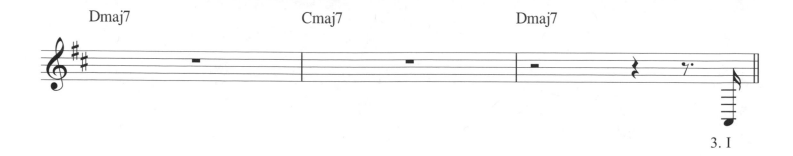

3. I

Verse

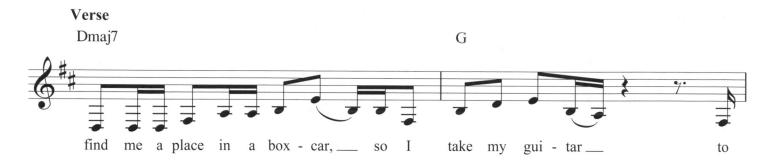

find me a place in a box-car, __ so I take my gui-tar __ to

pass some time. _____

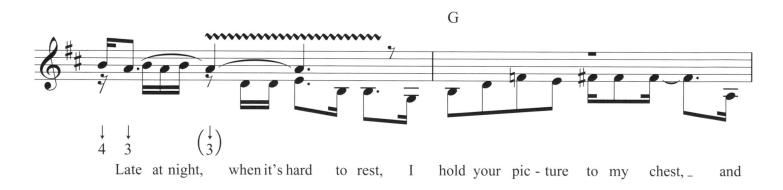

Late at night, when it's hard to rest, I hold your pic-ture to my chest, __ and

I feel __ fine. __

Chorus

But it's a rain-y night in ___ Geor - gia, ___   ba-by, it's a rain-y night in _

___ Geor - gia. _   I feel it's rain-in' all o - ver the world.   Kind - a lone-

w/ vocal ad lib till fade

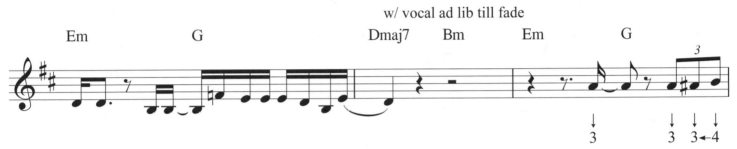

ly now,   and it's ___ rain-in' all o - ver the world... _

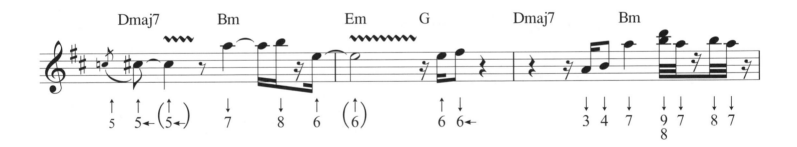

Begin fade

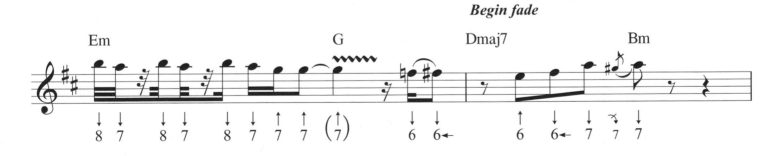

Fade out

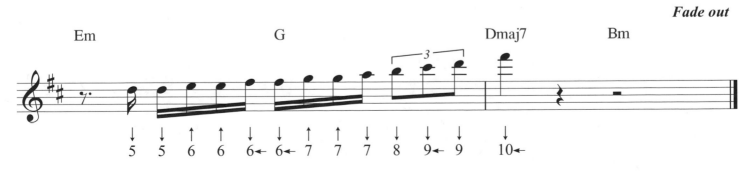

37

CHROMATIC HARMONICA NOTATION LEGEND

Harmonica music can be notated two different ways: on a *musical staff*, and in *tablature*.

THE MUSICAL STAFF shows pitches and rhythms and is divided by bar lines into measures. Pitches are named after the first seven letters of the alphabet.

TABLATURE graphically represents the harmonica music. Each note will be accompanied by a number, 1 through 12, indicating what hole you are to play. The arrow above indicates whether to blow or draw. (All examples are shown using a C chromatic harmonica.)

Blow (exhale) into 2nd hole.

Draw (inhale) 2nd & 3rd holes together.

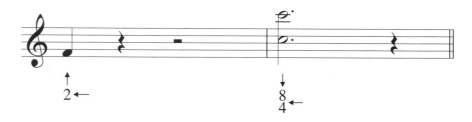

Blow into 2nd hole while holding the slide in.

Draw 4th & 8th holes together while holding the slide in.

Notes on the 12-Hole C Chromatic Harmonica

Exhaled (Blown) Notes with Slide Out

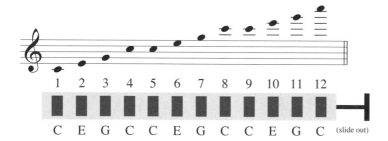

Inhaled (Drawn) Notes with Slide Out

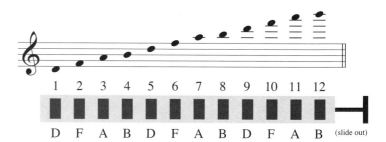

Exhaled (Blown) Notes with Slide In

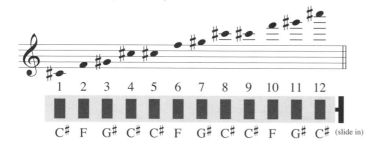

Inhaled (Drawn) Notes with Slide In

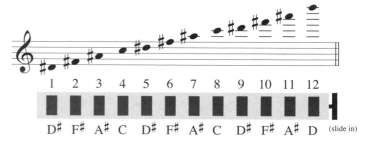

Definitions for Special Harmonica Notation

VIBRATO: Begin adding vibrato to the sustained note on beat 3.

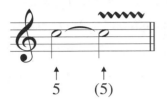

5   (5)

TONGUE BLOCKING: Using your tongue to block holes 2 & 3, play octaves on holes 1 & 4.

4
1

TRILL: Shake the harmonica rapidly to alternate between notes.

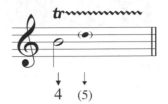

4   (5)

NOTE: Tablature numbers in parentheses are used when:
- The note is sustained, but a new articulation begins (such as vibrato), or
- The quantity of notes being sustained changes, or
- A change in dynamics (volume) occurs.
- It's the alternate note in a trill.

Additional Musical Definitions

D.S. al Coda
- Go back to the sign (𝄋), then play until the measure marked "***To Coda***," then skip to the section labelled "**Coda**."

D.C. al Fine
- Go back to the beginning of the song and play until the measure marked "***Fine***" (end).

- Repeat measures between signs.

 *(accent)*
- Accentuate the note (play initial attack louder).

 *(staccato)*
- Play the note short.

- When a repeated section has different endings, play the first ending only the first time and the second ending only the second time.

Dynamics

p
- Piano (soft)

mp
- Mezzo Piano (medium soft)

mf
- Mezzo Forte (medium loud)

f
- Forte (loud)

(crescendo) • Gradually louder

(decrescendo) • Gradually softer

HARMONICA PLAY-ALONG

AUDIO ACCESS INCLUDED

Play your favorite songs quickly and easily!

Just follow the notation, listen to the audio to hear how the harmonica should sound, and then play along using the separate full-band backing tracks. The melody and lyrics are also included in the book in case you want to sing, or to simply help you follow along. The audio CD is playable on any CD player. For PC and Mac computer users, the CD is enhanced so you can adjust the recording to any tempo without changing pitch!

1. Pop/Rock
And When I Die • Bright Side of the Road • I Should Have Known Better • Low Rider • Miss You • Piano Man • Take the Long Way Home • You Don't Know How It Feels.
00000478................$14.99

2. Rock Hits
Cowboy • Hand in My Pocket • Karma Chameleon • Middle of the Road • Run Around • Smokin' in the Boys Room • Train in Vain • What I like About You.
00000479................$14.99

3. Blues/Rock
Big Ten Inch Record • On the Road Again • Roadhouse Blues • Rollin' and Tumblin' • Train Kept A-Rollin' • Train, Train • Waitin' for the Bus • You Shook Me.
00000481................$14.99

4. Folk/Rock
Blowin' in the Wind • Catch the Wind • Daydream • Eve of Destruction • Me and Bobby McGee • Mr. Tambourine Man • Pastures of Plenty.
00000482................$14.99

5. Country Classics
Blue Bayou • Don't Tell Me Your Troubles • He Stopped Loving Her Today • Honky Tonk Blues • If You've Got the Money (I've Got the Time) • The Only Daddy That Will Walk the Line • Orange Blossom Special • Whiskey River.
00001004................$14.99

6. Country Hits
Ain't Goin' down ('Til the Sun Comes Up) • Drive (For Daddy Gene) • Getcha Some • Here's a Quarter (Call Someone Who Cares) • Honkytonk U • One More Last Chance • Put Yourself in My Shoes • Turn It Loose.
00001013................$14.99

8. Pop Classics
Bluesette • Cherry Pink and Apple Blossom White • From Me to You • Love Me Do • Midnight Cowboy • Moon River • Peg O' My Heart • A Rainy Night in Georgia.
00001090................$14.99

9. Chicago Blues
Blues with a Feeling • Easy • Got My Mo Jo Working • Help Me • I Ain't Got You • Juke • Messin' with the Kid.
00001091................$14.99

10. Blues Classics
Baby, Scratch My Back • Eyesight to the Blind • Good Morning Little Schoolgirl • Honest I Do • I'm Your Hoochie Coochie Man • My Babe • Ride and Roll • Sweet Home Chicago.
00001093................$14.99

11. Christmas Carols
Angels We Have Heard on High • Away in a Manger • Deck the Hall • The First Noel • Go, Tell It on the Mountain • Jingle Bells • Joy to the World • O Little Town of Bethlehem.
00001296................$12.99

12. Bob Dylan
All Along the Watchtower • Blowin' in the Wind • It Ain't Me Babe • Just like a Woman • Mr. Tambourine Man • Shelter from the Storm • Tangled up in Blue • The Times They Are A-Changin'.
00001326 ....$16.99

13. Little Walter
Can't Hold Out Much Longer • Crazy Legs • I Got to Go • Last Night • Mean Old World • Rocker • Sad Hours • You're So Fine.
00001334 ....$14.99

14. Jazz Standards
Autumn Leaves • Georgia on My Mind • Lullaby of Birdland • Meditation (Meditacao) • My Funny Valentine • Satin Doll • Some Day My Prince Will Come • What a Wonderful World.
00001335................$16.99

15. Jazz Classics
All Blues • Au Privave • Comin' Home Baby • Song for My Father • Sugar • Sunny • Take Five • Work Song.
00001336 ....$14.99

16. Christmas Favorites
Blue Christmas • Frosty the Snow Man • Here Comes Santa Claus (Right down Santa Claus Lane) • Jingle-Bell Rock • Nuttin' for Christmas • Rudolph the Red-Nosed Reindeer • Santa Claus Is Comin' to Town • Silver Bells.
00001350................$14.99

HAL•LEONARD®
Visit Hal Leonard Online
at **www.halleonard.com**

Prices, content, and availability subject to change without notice.

1217